MARJORIE KANN JACKSON

THE UNAVOIDABLE CHOICE

Stillwater Books
A Division of Sycamore Creek Press
Fort Worth, Texas
stillwaterbooksus.com

We want to hear from you. Please visit us at Stillwaterbooksus.com or on our Facebook site, Stillwaterbooks.

Stillwater Books
A Division of Sycamore Creek Press
Fort Worth, Texas
stillwaterbooksus.com

The Unavoidable Choice

Cover art and design: Lynn Jackson Talley

This book is also available on Kindle through Amazon.com.

Library of Congress Cataloging Publication Data
Jackson, Marjorie Kann.
The Unavoidable Choice/ Marjorie Kann Jackson
1st ed.
p. cm.
ISBN-13: 978-1514190487
1. Christian Living/Inspirational

First edition, Stillwater Books 2015
Printed in the United States of America

In loving memory of my husband

James Weldon Jackson

1933-2014

And with grateful thanksgiving to God
for the sixty years we shared.

Love is Eternal.
May God increase our love.

THERE IS A CHOICE YOU WILL MAKE,

AND THERE IS NO WAY TO AVOID IT.

IT WILL DETERMINE

HOW YOU LIVE ON THIS EARTH,

AS WELL AS

WHERE YOU WILL SPEND ETERNITY.

THERE ARE ONLY

TWO WAYS LIFE CAN BE LIVED -

YOUR WAY,

WHICH THE BIBLE TELLS US

IS THE WAY OF DEATH,

OR GOD'S WAY,

WHICH THE BIBLE TELLS US

IS THE WAY OF LIFE.

WHICH WILL YOU CHOOSE?

HOW WILL YOU EXPERIENCE

THE CONSEQUENCES OF YOUR CHOICE?

Valentines Day of 2014 was the last normal day my husband, James, and I shared. The next morning, he had a fall that led to his move to heaven on February 21st. He had been on hospice care for almost nine months. On March 1st, the day before our fifty-eighth wedding anniversary, we held his memorial service.

The evening before his fall we shared a conversation about issues of life and death. For most of our married life I taught a weekly Bible class, while he served on church and ministry boards. That evening we talked about what it means to be born again of the Spirit of God. We agreed that many people reject Christianity because it doesn't make sense to them, and that many life-long church members live with unanswered questions. **What does it mean** to be born again? **What is** born again? **Why** do we have to be born again? **What does that change? How does a new birth play out** in everyday life? **How does it determine our eternal destination?** After he was gone, I prepared this treatise to bring clarity and assurance to the hearts of others and to encourage them to consider the unavoidable choice. Everything written in italics is taken from the Holy Bible.

GOD KNOWS YOU AND HE LOVES YOU

God created you to have a personal relationship with Him. *"You made all the delicate, inner parts of my body and knit them together in my mother's womb. You were there while I was being formed in utter seclusion. You saw me before I was born and scheduled each day of my life before I began to breathe. Every day was recorded in your book!*

How precious it is, Lord, to realize that you are thinking about me constantly! I can't even count how many times a day your thoughts turn toward me. And when I waken in the morning, you are still thinking of me!" (Psalm 139: 13, 15-18).

Who is it that speaks these tender words of love? It is the God of the Bible, who made the heavens and earth. He is the ONE TRUE GOD whose life is expressed in three ways. The Bible refers to **God the Father, God the Son, and God the Holy Spirit.** In Matthew 28:19 Jesus spoke clearly the truth of His Life when He said to His disciples, *"All authority in heaven and on earth has been given to me. Therefore go and make disciples of all nations, baptizing them in the name of* ***the Father*** *and of* ***the Son*** (Jesus Christ) *and of* ***the Holy Spirit...***"

- ◆ What are your thoughts on God's desire to have a personal relationship with you? What are those thoughts based on?

YET GOD CANNOT ACCEPT YOU
AS YOU ARE

Why is this? It is because of sin. Sin is a word that is not used much anymore. Many people don't believe in sin. They believe that one person's values are just as good as another's; therefore, there is no such thing as sin. However, the Bible tells us that there are absolute values. The ability to distinguish between right and wrong is derived from who God is and what God says. The only standard by which moral values may be judged accurately is the holy character of God. In 1 John 1:8 we read, *"If we say we have no sin we deceive ourselves, and the truth is not in us."*

3

God has marked out moral boundaries that fulfill His Law of Love. They are for your good and His glory. The truth of the matter is that no matter how good you are, you can never measure up to God's standard. *"All have sinned and fall short of the glory of God"* (Romans 3:23). You fall short through what you think, what you say, and what you do. You also fall short by failing to do what you know you should do. *"Anyone, then, who knows the good he ought to do and doesn't do it, sins"* (James 4:17). In Isaiah 64:6 we read, *"All of us have become like one who is unclean, and all our righteous acts are like filthy rags."* In a modern translation of the Bible, The Message, this truth is expressed: *"It wasn't so long ago that you were mired in that old stagnant life of sin. You let the world, which doesn't know the first thing about living, tell you how to live. You filled your lungs with polluted unbelief, and then exhaled disobedience. We all did it, all of us doing what we felt like doing, when we felt like doing it, all of us in the same boat"* (Ephesians 2:1-3).

Where did sin come from? The first sin took place in heaven. It was committed by the highest and most exalted of all the angelic beings, Lucifer, whose name meant "son of the morning." We know him today as Satan. He determined in his heart that he would pursue his own course of independent action. His goal was to raise his throne above the throne of God. He believed that he could be like God! Many of the angels joined in his rebellion. You may read Satan's story in the Bible in Isaiah 14:12-14 and about the fallen angels in Jude 1:6.

How did sin come to earth? In the Old Testament, we read that God created the first man and woman, Adam (the forefather of the human race) and Eve. They were without sin, perfect beings made in the image of God. They lived in constant and joyful communion with God. They were not subject to death. However, sin came to planet earth **by way of Satan, and through Adam and Eve**. In the book of Genesis (chapters 2 and 3), we read that it was Satan who tempted Adam and Eve to re-enact on earth the sin which he had already orchestrated in heaven.

God had commanded them not to eat the fruit of the tree of the knowledge of good and evil; and warned them that if they ate of it, they would surely die. Satan told them that by eating of it, their eyes would be opened and they would be like God (Genesis 3:1-5).

This is Satan's lie, that you can be your own God. Now, he had proclaimed it to the universe! Planet earth is the stage on which the consequences of the lie are being played out. Ultimately it will be proved untrue. We have the promise found in Philippians 2:10 which says the day will come when, *"at the name of Jesus, every knee will bow, in heaven and on earth and under the earth, and every tongue confess that Jesus Christ is Lord, to the glory of God the Father."*

How does sin affect you? With sin came death. *"**For the wages of sin is death** . . ."* (Romans 6:23). *"There is a way that seems right to a man, but **its end is the way of death"** (Proverbs 18:12). Death is not extinction, but **separation.** There are **three kinds of death.** Physical death is separation of the soul and spirit from the body. Spiritual death is separation of the soul and spirit from God. The Bible also tells of "the second death", which is the eternal experience of death, in all of its forms, in the Lake of Fire. (See Revelation 21:8.) Adam's original sin is the one and only cause of death. How can that be?

Sin caused Adam and Eve to become **beings of a different order.** No longer filled with the Life of God, **they now had spirits that were dead and bodies that were dying.** They were no longer able to communicate with God. They no longer had eyes that could see, or ears that could hear, or hearts that could understand spiritual things, and they had a sin nature. What is a sin nature? It is a natural tendency, an inherent determination, to live life your own way. It is all in you that opposes the revealed will of God. This is the truth of our existence, for we are all born of the seed of Adam, sons and daughters made in Adam's image. *"This, then, is what has happened. **Sin made its entry into the**

world through one man, and through sin, death. The inheritance
of sin and death passed on to the whole human race, and no one
could break it for no one was himself free from sin" (Romans
5:12).

◆ What values do you live by? What do you base your
  values on?

◆ According to the Bible, how are moral values to be
  determined?

◆ Can you explain the nature of the first sin that took place in
  the universe? Where did it occur?

♦ In what ways are you able to see sin still running its course today? Examine your life to see if you are seeking to live free of any interference from God.

♦ How is it true that Adam's original sin is the only cause of death in all its forms?

♦ How did sin change Adam and Eve, and how has their original sin affected the whole human race?

HOWEVER, GOD HAS A DIVINE PLAN

It is not a list of rules to be followed, or a system of reform, or a set of beliefs. **It is not** a plan whereby we can earn our way to heaven. **It is not** a plan to rescue unfortunate human beings for their own sakes. **It is not** God's remedy for human failure. Rather, **it is a plan to fulfill God's eternal purpose** by demonstrating His full character to the entire universe. **It is a plan** that demonstrates His matchless love and His righteous judgement. **It is a plan** that will bring Him honor and glory throughout eternity. **It is a plan to redeem, a plan to buy back, a plan to recover those who are lost to God. It is a plan of salvation!** *"He destined us in love to be his sons through Jesus Christ, according to the purpose of his will, to the praise of his glorious grace which he freely bestowed on us in the Beloved"* (Ephesians 1:5-6).

It is a work of God for mankind. It is not a work of men for God. No one can make of himself a new creation. No one can forgive his own sins, or impart to himself eternal life, or clothe himself in the righteousness of God, or write his own name in heaven. God has the greatest of all motives, in that His plan satisfies the infinite love He has for those whose lives are ruined by sin. The salvation of a single soul means more to God than it will ever mean to the one who has been saved, for His matchless gift has been accepted. In Luke 15:10 Jesus said, *". . . there is rejoicing **in the presence of the angels** over one sinner who repents."*

It is a plan requiring that a ransom be paid, and only God could pay it. Why would a ransom be required? Romans 7:14 explains that it is because we are *"creatures of the flesh (carnal, unspiritual) having been sold into slavery under (the control of) sin."* **God the Son** would lay aside His rights as God and leave the glories of heaven in order to ransom you. He would take on a human body and then He would die a terrible death to make it possible for you to live forever with Him in heaven. **The Son of**

God, the Lord Jesus Christ, **would lay down His Life on the cross of Calvary in order to pay for your sins, and for the sins of all who accept His gift of grace.** This was the greatest sacrifice the universe has ever witnessed! Amazing love! How can it be, that Thou my God should die for me?

I love the way J.B. Phillips translated this truth, as it is found in Philippians 2:5-10. *"He who had always been God by nature, did not cling to His privileges as God's equal, but stripped Himself of every advantage by consenting to be a slave by nature* (Note: a slave to His Father; NEVER a slave of men) *and being born a man. And, plainly seen as a human being, He humbled Himself by living a life of utter obedience, to the point of death, and the death He died was the death of a common criminal. That is why God has now lifted Him to the heights, and has given Him the name beyond all names, so that at the name of Jesus every knee shall bow, whether in heaven or earth or under the earth. And that is why every tongue shall confess that Jesus Christ is Lord, to the glory of God the Father."*

◆ What is God's purpose for His plan of redemption?

◆ Why does redemption have to be a work of God for mankind, and not a work of men for God?

HOW WOULD GOD'S PLAN
BE FULFILLED?

By the death of Jesus Christ, God disposed of that which is evil. He conquered death and offers you His life! *"He Himself bore our sins in His body on the tree, so that we might die to sins and live for righteousness,* for by His wounds you have been healed"* (1 Peter 2:24). *"For you know that it was not with perishable things such as silver or gold that **you were redeemed** from the empty way of life handed down to you from your forefathers, but with the precious blood of Christ, a lamb without blemish or defect. He was chosen before the creation of the world, but was revealed in these last times for your sake"* (1 Peter 1:18-20).

Through giving you a new birth, God would secure that which is good. In John 3 Jesus told Nicodemus that His plan for mankind could only be accomplished through a new birth by which they could be made over in the image of God. Through the rebirth of their spirits, men would be empowered by a new dynamic, the life of God Himself! Colossians 1:27 tells us that this new life is actually, *"**Christ in you, the hope of glory.**"* In John 3:3 Jesus likened it to *"**being born from above**".* Jesus said in John 10:1, *"**I have come that they might have life,** and that they might have it more abundantly."* God would begin with those who are perfectly lost and utterly condemned and bring them into Christ-likeness. There has never been a greater miracle in the entire universe!

In 31 AD a ruler of the Jews named Nicodemus came to talk to Jesus. Jesus said to him, *"With all the earnestness I possess I tell you this: Unless you are born again, you can never get into the Kingdom of God."*

"Born again!" exclaimed Nicodemus. *"What do you mean? How can an old man go back into his mother's womb and be born again?"*

Jesus replied, "What I am telling you so earnestly is this: Unless one is born of water (a natural birth)*, and of the Spirit* (a spiritual rebirth)*, he cannot enter the Kingdom of God. Men can only reproduce human life* (flesh gives birth to flesh)*, but the Holy Spirit gives new life from heaven* (spirit gives birth to spirit)*; so don't be surprised at my statement that you must be born again"* (John 3:3-7).

◆   What does being born again mean to you? How would you explain it to someone else?

HOW IMPORTANT IS ALL OF THIS?

Jesus said "I am the way and the truth and the life. No one comes to the Father except through me" (John 14:6). According to the Bible, there will be no one in heaven who has not been born again of the Spirit of God. There are many terms used that all refer to this wonderful event. It is referred to as "salvation", as being "saved", as "belonging to Christ", or as "becoming a Christian". Jesus referred to it as "being born again".

In Acts 4:12 we read, **"Salvation is found in no one else,** *for there is no other name under heaven given to men by which we must be saved."* 1 Timothy 2:5 states, *"For there is **one God** and **one mediator between God and men, the man Christ Jesus who gave Himself as a ransom** for all men . . ."*

HOW CAN THIS NEW LIFE
BECOME YOURS?

This new life becomes yours when you accept the testimony of God's Word, which says that you stand before God spiritually dead and physically dying. You are a dead person walking, and the Bible tells you there is nothing you can do about it other than to throw yourself on God's love and mercy. *"As for you, you were dead in your transgressions and sins, in which you used to live when you followed the ways of this world and of the ruler of the kingdom of the air, the spirit who is now at work in those who are disobedient. All of us also lived among them at one time, gratifying the cravings of our sinful nature and following its desires and thoughts. Like the rest, we were by nature objects of* (God's) *wrath"* (Ephesians 2:1-3).

The Bible describes eternal life as a remarkable parallel of earthly life. When a baby is conceived, a new being originates. It did not exist before, and it will live on forever. Likewise, in spiritual regeneration, through divine re-creation, a new being comes into existence that did not exist before. First, there is the Seed of Life. There is the meeting of two living substances. One is aggressive and the other is receptive.

With spiritual rebirth, the aggressive element is the living and active Word of God. It is through His Word that God enters human life. My mother taught that God always speaks loudly enough for a listening heart to hear! *"For you have been born again, not of perishable seed, but of imperishable, through the living and enduring word of God"* (1 Peter 1:23).

The receptive element is the human spirit. *"Yet to all who received Him, to those who believed in His name, He gave the right to become children of God – children born not of natural descent, nor of human decision or a husband's will, but born of God"* (John 1: 12-13).

The moment you decide to accept God's matchless gift of Life, **you are given the faith God requires to receive it.** It is not mere intellectual assent. It is active reliance on the truth of God's Word. Saving faith is not something you must try to conjure up within yourself. It is the gift of God! *"For it is by grace you have been saved, through faith – and this* (faith) *is not from yourselves, it is the gift of God; not by works so that no one can boast"* (Ephesians 2:8-9).

You can pray this simple prayer. . . "Dear God, I want to be born again, born into Your family. Right now, I choose to accept your gift of a new life. Thank You Jesus, for making that possible! In Your name I pray, Amen. So be it!"

In Acts 16:31 we read, *"Believe on the Lord Jesus Christ and you shall be saved."* The new birth is so simple to understand and receive that even a child can act on it and fully accept it. However, it is so profound that we will be plumbing the depths of its truth throughout eternity.

"It was through what His Son did, that God cleared a path for everything to come to Him – all things in heaven and on earth – for Christ's death on the cross has made peace with God for all by His blood. This includes you who were once far away from God. You were His enemies and hated Him and were separated from Him by your evil thoughts and actions, yet now He has brought you back as His friends. He has done this through the death on the cross of His own human body, and now as a result, Christ has brought you into the very presence of God, and you are standing there before Him with nothing left against you – nothing that He could even chide you for. The only condition is that you fully believe the Truth, standing in it steadfast and firm, strong in the Lord, convinced of the Good News that Jesus died for you, and never shifting from trusting Him to save you" (Colossians 1:20-23).

In the New Testament, there are at least 150 passages which declare that the **new birth is received by faith alone.** In no way does it rest on your works. It is not a matter of pleading with God for mercy and salvation. It is not a matter of believing **plus** repenting, of believing **plus** confessing Christ, of believing **plus** being baptized, of believing **plus** taking communion, of believing **plus** surrender to God, or of believing **plus** the confession of sin. Confession, repentance, surrender, baptism, and communion are all integral parts of **living** and **growing** in the Christian life. As you enter into them, you will have to adjust yourself to God's mercy; for through these avenues, all of His blessings await your willingness to gratefully receive what He has already provided. However, they are not a necessary part of **the birth process.** *"For God so loved the world that He gave His one and only Son, that* ***whosoever believes in Him shall not perish*** *but have eternal life. For God did not send His Son into the world to condemn the world, but to save the world through Him"* (John 3:16-17).

There is a moment of birth! Spirit gives birth to spirit. You have been born as a babe in Christ. As surely as a human baby possesses human life, **you now possess the Life of God. You are a new creation.** *"Therefore, if anyone is in Christ, he is a new creation; the old has gone, the new has come!"* (2 Corinthians 5:17). It takes only moments to receive this new life, and it can never be taken from you. Just as you can never be unborn physically, so you can never be unborn spiritually. You may disappoint or grieve or disgrace your Heavenly Father. Fellowship with Him can be broken, and that can lead to the experience of His chastisement; but you can never be unborn.

"Don't cause the Holy Spirit sorrow by the way you live. Remember, He is the one who marks you to be present on that day when salvation from sin will be complete. Stop being mean, bad-tempered and angry. Quarreling, harsh words, and dislike of others should have no place in your lives. Instead, be kind to each other, tender-hearted, forgiving one another, just as God has forgiven you because you belong to Christ" (Ephesians 4:30-32).

A newborn baby knows nothing of the life that lies before him. As yet, he has no capacity for understanding such things; but he possesses life and the capacity to grow and mature. Neither can the scope of eternal life be perceived at the time of spiritual rebirth. The truth is that a Christian is much more than a forgiven sinner. The Bible describes 33 works of God that take place instantaneously and simultaneously on your behalf when you are born again. (See addendum.) They make up one complete whole and cannot be separated. Not one can be claimed alone!

These works are grounded on the merit of the Lord Jesus Christ; therefore, they are yours for eternity. The full realization of the Life that is now yours awaits the day of God's choosing. *"Beloved, now we are children of God, and what we will be has not yet been made known. But we know that when He appears, **we shall be like Him,** for we shall see Him as He is"* (1 John 3:2).

◆ Can you explain how spiritual life is a parallel of earthly life?

◆ What must you believe in order to be "born again"? What kind of faith is required in order to receive this gift of God?

◆ Can you explain the new life you receive when you are born again? Is it possible to ever lose that life?

IF YOU ACCEPT THIS NEW LIFE
WHAT HAPPENS TO YOU?

No longer are you dead in sin. Death in all its forms has been overcome by Life! **No longer are you separated from God**. You can begin to share God's life here and now, as you read the Bible and pray to Him. *"But now in Christ Jesus you who once were far away have been brought near through the blood of Christ"* (Ephesians 2:13).

All of your sins have been forgiven - past, present, and future. God will never bring a charge against you! This is a one-time forgiveness of God that is part of your new birth. Human forgiveness overlooks what is owed. Divine forgiveness can be offered because the debt owed was paid in full. Jesus paid it all! *"Therefore, there is now no condemnation for those who are in Christ Jesus"* (Romans 8:1).

My dad used to illustrate what it means to be "in Christ" by holding up his Bible and stating that it represented Jesus Christ. Then he would take a small piece of paper and explain that the paper represented him, Herbert Kann. Placing the paper in the Bible and closing it, he would demonstrate that the paper could no longer be seen. He would conclude by saying that this is how God sees you, once you have been born again. When God looks at you, He sees Jesus! *"It is because of God that you are **in Christ Jesus,*** *who has become for us, wisdom from God – that is, our righteousness, holiness, and redemption"* (1 Corinthians 1:30).

Not only are your sins forgiven so that you do not have to pay the penalty for them, but you are separated from them. The words that are often translated "forgiveness" in the Bible, mean "to send away". *"As far as the east is from the west, so far has He removed our transgressions from us* (Psalm 103:12).

Forgiveness subtracts from your life what was sinful. **Justification adds** to your life the righteousness of Christ. *"He (Jesus) was delivered over to death for our sins and was raised to life for our justification"* (Romans 4:25). *"May I be found in Him, not having a righteousness that comes from the law, but that which is through faith in Christ – the righteousness that comes from God and is by faith"* (Philippians 3:9).

God has made every possible provision for you! **You have an advocate** with the Father, Jesus Christ, who prays for you. In Hebrews 7:25 we read, *"He (Jesus Christ) is able to save completely those who come to God through Him, because He always **lives to intercede** for them."* Also, Romans 8:34 states, *"Christ Jesus, who died – more than that, who was raised to life – is at the right hand of God and is **also interceding** for us."* Romans 8:26-27 states that, *"And in the same way – by our faith – the Holy Spirit helps us with our daily problems and in our praying. For we don't even know what we should pray for, nor how to pray as we should; but **the Holy Spirit prays for us** with such feeling that it cannot be expressed in words. And the Father who knows all hearts knows, of course, what the Spirit is saying as He pleads for us in harmony with God's own will."*

You receive a new nature through the gift of the Holy Spirit. *"His divine power has given us everything we need for life and godliness through our knowledge of Him who called us by His own glory and goodness. Through these He has given us His great* *and precious promises, so that through them you may participate in the divine nature and escape the corruption in the world caused by evil desires"* (2 Peter 1:3-4).

You have the incredible opportunity of growing up into Christ! *"Like newborn babies, crave pure spiritual milk, so that by it you may grow up in your salvation"* (1Peter 2:2). *"Then we will no longer be infants, tossed back and forth by the waves, and blown here and there by every wind of teaching and by the cunning and craftiness of men in their deceitful scheming. Instead, speaking the truth in love, we will in all things grow up into Him who is the Head, that is, Christ"* (Ephesians 4:14-15).

Finally, God has a wonderful plan for your life! *"For I know the plans I have for you, declares the Lord, "plans to prosper you and not to harm you, plans to give you hope and a future"* (Jeremiah 29:11). God has now begun a good work in you, and He promises to bring it to completion. You can be confident of this very thing, *"that He who began a good work in you will carry it on to completion until the day of Christ Jesus"* (Philippians 1:6). *"After you have suffered a little while, our God, who is full of kindness through Christ, **will give you His eternal glory.** He personally will come and pick you up, and set you firmly in place and make you stronger than ever. To Him be all power over all things, forever and ever, Amen"* (1 Peter 5:10-11).

◆ How does your new birth deal with sin and death?

♦ What sins are covered by God's forgiveness? How does God's forgiveness differ from human forgiveness?

♦ What is the significance of being separated from your sin?

♦ What blessing can you discover in the truth that forgiveness subtracts from your life and justification adds to your life?

◆ What do you think it means to have an advocate with the Father?

◆ How do you receive a new nature? What difference will it make in how you live and experience your life?

◆ What do you think it means to grow up into Christ?

YET YOU STILL SIN

That is true, and God anticipated your ongoing sin. God knew that once you were born again your walk with Him in this world would not be perfect. As long as you live on earth, you will live in the body of sin that you inherited from Adam, in a body that is dying and that still contains, along with your new nature, a sin nature. The apostle Paul wrote about this in Romans 7:15. *"It is a fact of life that when I want to do what is right, I inevitably do what is wrong. I love to do God's will so far as my new nature is concerned; but there is something else deep within me in my lower nature, that is at war with my mind and wins the fight and makes me a slave to the sin that is still within me. In my mind I want to be God's willing servant but instead I find myself still enslaved to sin. So you see how it is; my new life tells me to do right, but the old nature that is still inside me loves to sin. Oh, what a terrible predicament I'm in! Who will free me from my slavery to this deadly lower nature? Thank God! It has been done by Jesus Christ our Lord. He has set me free."*

When your relationship with God is disrupted by sin, God provides ongoing forgiveness and ongoing cleansing; but you must acknowledge and confess your sin, and you must repent of it. You must stop doing it! This is the one and only way a child of God can be restored to fellowship with his Heavenly Father. 1 John 1:9 states that, *"If we confess our sins, He is faithful and just to forgive us our sins, and to cleanse us from all unrighteousness."* All of God's forgiveness is based on the shed blood of the Lord Jesus Christ. What your forgiveness cost God cannot be fathomed by the human mind!

♦ Can you explain why it is that you continue to sin?

◆ What is the connection that exists between ongoing confession and ongoing forgiveness? Why is this important for a child of God?

HOWEVER, THE HOLY SPIRIT
IS NOW YOUR HELPER

God also knew that you would need the presence and the ongoing power of the Holy Spirit to live the Christian life. This is why when Jesus left this world and returned to heaven, He asked His Father to send the Holy Spirit to be with you and to live in you and through you. This marked THE GRAND CULMINATION of Jesus' mission to earth! *"I will ask the Father, and He will give you another Counselor, the Spirit of truth, to be with you forever. The world cannot accept this Counselor, because it neither sees Him nor knows Him. But you know Him, for He lives with you and will be in you"* (John 14:16-17). The Holy Spirit brings to you the will and the power to live this new life. In Luke 1:74-75 we read that, *"He will enable us to serve Him without fear in holiness and righteousness before Him all our days."*

Much of the secret of **the workings of the Holy Spirit** in and through the life of born again believers is simply a matter of becoming aware of Him. That awareness begins with an attitude of belief in what we read in God's Word. The Holy Spirit quietly comes to make His home in our spirits. In the process He transforms us, as we gladly choose to open ourselves to His residency. *"But **the fruit of the Spirit** is love, joy, peace, patience, kindness, goodness, faithfulness, gentleness and self-control. Against such things there is no law"* (Galatians 5:22-23).

◆ How is it that the coming of the Holy Spirit marks the high point of Jesus' mission to mankind? What does His coming bring to your life?

HOW CAN YOU BE ASSURED THAT YOU HAVE TRULY RECEIVED A NEW LIFE?

You know you have received a new life because God says so! *"When the kindness and love of God our Savior appeared, He saved us, not because of righteous things we had done, but because of His mercy. He saved us through the washing of rebirth and renewal by the Holy Spirit, whom He poured out on us generously through Jesus Christ our Savior, so that, having been justified by His grace we might become heirs having the hope of eternal life"* (Titus 3:5–7). Romans 8:16 tells us that, *"The Spirit Himself testifies with our spirit that we are God's children. Now if we are children, then we are heirs – heirs of God and co-heirs with Christ..."*

It is also true that the life that is in you will continue to develop, and is the life that will be expressed through you. Progressively you will reveal what you are and whose you are. *"Do you want more and more of God's kindness and peace? Then learn to know Him better and better. For as you know Him better, he will give you, through His great power, everything you need for living a truly good life. . ."* (2 Peter 1:2-3).

♦ How can you know for sure that you have been born from above?

IF YOU HAVE RECEIVED THIS NEW LIFE, IT NEEDS TO GROW STRONG WITHIN YOU

You must provide the elements necessary for growth; however, as is true in every realm, it is God who provides growth. Talk to God every day. He is with you now, a participating presence in your life. Read the Bible as if it were written just for you. You may want to read only until a verse speaks to your heart. Then stop. Underline it. Write it out, and think about it throughout the day. You may want to begin reading with the book of John or the short books of Ephesians, Philippians, or Colossians. It is of great benefit to keep a journal. If you choose to do even some of these things, you cannot help but grow spiritually and you will not be able to stop growing! My mother, Dr. Margaret Kann, wrote in her Bible that "to grow spiritually is the most wonderful becoming that is possible for a human being to experience."

Bear witness to your faith. Share with others what you have done. Faith begins in your thoughts, and is lived out through your words and your actions. *"Let your light so shine before men, that they may see your good works and give glory to your Father who is in heaven"* (Matthew 5:16).

Find a church or a Bible study group where you can share fellowship with other believers. *"I ask Him* (the Father) *to strengthen you by His Spirit - not a brute strength but a glorious inner strength - that Christ will live in you as you open the door and invite him in. And I ask Him that with both feet planted firmly on love, you'll be able to take in with all Christians the extravagant dimensions of Christ's love. Reach out and experience the breadth! Test its length! Plumb the depths! Rise to the heights! Live full lives, full in the fullness of God. God can do anything, you know - far more than you could ever imagine or guess or request in your wildest dreams! He does it not by pushing us around but by working within us, His Spirit deeply and gently within us"* (Ephesians 3: 17-19).

◆ What responsibility do you bear in order to grow stronger spiritually? How can you carry this out? In what ways can your life be enriched through fellowship with other believers?

AND THE BEST IS YET TO COME!

The resurrection of Jesus was not merely the reversal of death. When He arose, He was not the same order of being He had been before His crucifixion. He is the only person who has ever risen from the dead with a glorified body! He is the only being in the universe with a glorified body and His resurrection body is the pattern for the body you will one day have in heaven. He arose as the Head of a new race! In 1 Corinthians 15:50 Paul writes, *"I tell you this, my brothers: an earthly body made of flesh and blood cannot get into God's kingdom. These perishable bodies of ours are not the right kind to live forever."* In Philippians 3:20-21 we read, *"But our citizenship is in heaven. And we eagerly await a Savior from there, the Lord Jesus Christ, who by the power that enables Him to bring everything under His control, will transform our lowly bodies so that they will be like His glorious body."* You may learn more about this in 1 Corinthians 15. It is awesome!

You are being prepared for an ongoing life in heaven. Heaven is being populated by those who, in his life, were born again of the Spirit of God. When you die, you will join your loved ones and the born again of all the ages and, *"so we will be with the Lord forever. Therefore encourage each other with these words"* (1 Thessalonians 4:17-18). In John 14:1-3 we read, *"Do not let your hearts be troubled. Trust in God, trust also in me. In my Father's house are many rooms; if it were not so, I would have told you. I am going there to prepare a place for you. And if I go and prepare a place for you, I will come back and take you to be with me, that you also may be where I am."* We also have the promise found in I Corinthians 2:9: *"Eye has not seen, nor ear heard, nor has entered into the heart of man the things which God has prepared for those who love Him."*

♦ What significance does it have for your future that Jesus rose from the dead with a glorified body? Can you explain what it means that Jesus arose as the head of a new race?

WHAT WILL HAPPEN IF YOU REJECT GOD'S GIFT OF A NEW BIRTH?

The Bible makes it clear that **all people will not be in heaven**, and the Bible holds out no hope that those who reject God's grace and provision will have an opportunity to accept it in a future existence. The sacrifice of Jesus Christ stands as the basis for a greater condemnation on those who choose to reject the remedy that is provided by God's infinite love. The Bible tells us that those who reject God's salvation go to hell. **God does not send anyone to hell. Always, that is the individual's choice.** The wonder is not that sinners are eternally lost, but that they are ever saved.

Hell is the most solemn doctrine in the entire Bible. The human mind is revolted by the very idea of it, but the idea of hell did not originate with human reason. Most references to hell that are found in the Bible come from Jesus Himself. In fact, Jesus spoke more of hell than He did of heaven. He alone reveals this place, and hell is a real place! **Hell is presented as the final place in which God deals with those who are eternally lost.**

While heaven is a place of eternal life, hell is **a place of eternal death.** That means that it is a place in which **all three kinds of death are experienced forever and ever.** Remember that death is separation. Hell is a place of total separation, not only from God, but from each other. It is a place of complete isolation from all you ever knew and loved. In the Bible, we are told that **hell is a place of unending torment.** It is further described as **a place of outer darkness where,** *"there will be weeping and gnashing of teeth"* (Matthew 13:42). **It is a place where** *"the smoke of their torment ascendeth up forever and ever; and they have no rest day nor night"* (Revelation 14:11). **It is a place of everlasting fire** (Matthew 25:41). These verses attempt to put into language, truths that are beyond the power of words to describe! Read the story Jesus told of the rich man and the beggar. It is found in Luke 16:19-31.

There is no place in the Bible that suggests there will ever be an end to conscious existence in either heaven or hell. *"He that believes on the Son has everlasting life: and he that believes not the Son shall not see life; but the wrath of God abides on him"* (John 3:36).

There are those who say there cannot be a hell because God is a God of love. At this point, human opinion intrudes into areas about which it has no knowledge. People who say such things understand nothing of the depth and depravity of sin or of the utter holiness and justice of God. There are realities in the universe that man will never comprehend, **but a precedent has been set**. A loving God created the hosts of angels, yet they are given no second chance, and there is no redemption offered for those who, in following Lucifer, fell from grace. *"Then He* (the King, the Son of Man) *will say to those on his left, 'Depart from me you who are cursed, into the eternal fire prepared for the devil and his angels'"* (Matthew 25:41).

So here you have it . . . **the unavoidable choice** every human being faces. You were born into death, but you can choose life!

- ◆ Do you believe you will go to heaven when you die? What is the basis for your belief?

◆ How does the Bible describe everlasting death and everlasting life?

◆ What is **your choice**?

"I call heaven and earth as witnesses today against you,

for I have set before you life and death,

the blessing and the curse;

therefore choose life,

that both you and your descendants may live;

that you may love the Lord your God,

that you may obey His voice,

and that you may cling to Him,

for He is your life and the length of your days . . ."

Deuteronomy 30:19-20

Written by Marjorie Kann Jackson
2014 -2015

If this has been helpful to you, please share it with someone. Scripture verses were drawn from several translations of the Bible: The King James Translation, The Message, the Revised Standard Version, the Living Bible, the New International Version, and the J.B.Phillips Translation, and were chosen for clarity.

THIRTY- THREE WORKS OF GOD
THAT COMPRISE
THE SALVATION OF A SOUL

1. I AM IN THE ETERNAL PLAN OF GOD.
    (Acts 2:23; 1 Peter 1:2, 20)

2. I AM REDEEMED.
    (Galatians 5:1, Romans 3:24)

3. I AM RECONCILED TO GOD.
    (2 Corinthians 5:19-21)

4. I AM RELATED TO GOD THROUGH PROPITIATION.
    (1 John 2:2)

5. I AM FORGIVEN OF ALL TRESPASSES.
    (Colossians 2:13, Ephesians 1:7, Colossians 1:14)

6. I AM VITALLY JOINED WITH CHRIST IN THE DEATH OF MY SIN NATURE.
    (Romans 6:1–10, Galatians 2:20)

7. I AM SET FREE FROM THE LAW.
    (John 1:17, Acts 15:24-29, Romans 6:14)

8. I AM A CHILD OF GOD.
    (John 3:6, John 1:12-13, 1 Peter 1:23)

9. I AM ADOPTED INTO GOD'S FAMILY.
    (Ephesians 1:4-5, Romans 8:23)

10. I AM ACCEPTABLE TO GOD BY JESUS CHRIST.
    (Ephesians 1:6, 1 Peter 2:5, 1 Corinthians 1:30)

11.   I AM JUSTIFIED BY GOD.
(Romans 4:5, 5:1)

12.   I AM MADE NEAR TO GOD.
(Ephesians 2:13)

13.   I AM DELIVERED FROM THE POWER OF DARKNESS.
(Colossians 1:13, 2 Corinthians 4:3-4)

14.   I AM PLACED INTO THE KINGDOM OF THE SON OF HIS LOVE.
(Colossians 1:13, 1 Thessalonians 2:12)

15.   I AM ESTABLISHED ON THE ROCK, CHRIST JESUS.
(1 Corinthians 3:9-15, Matthew 7:24-27)

16.   I AM A GIFT FROM GOD THE FATHER TO CHRIST.
(John 17:13)

17.   I AM CIRCUMCISED IN CHRIST.
(Ephesians 2:11, Colossians 2:11)

18.   I AM PART OF THE HOLY AND ROYAL PRIEST-HOOD.
(1 Peter 2:5)

19.   I AM CHOSEN, HOLY, PECULIAR, DIFFERENT.
(1 Peter 2:9)

20.   I AM A CITIZEN OF HEAVEN.
(Philippians 3:20)

21.   I AM OF THE FAMILY AND HOUSEHOLD OF GOD.
(Ephesians 2:19, Galatians 6:10)

22.   I AM IN THE FELLOWSHIP OF THE SAINTS.
       (John 17:21-23)

23.   I HAVE A HEAVENLY ASSOCIATION.
       (Colossians 3:1)

24.   I HAVE ACCESS TO GOD.
       (Hebrews 4:16)

25.   I LIVE WITHIN THE MUCH MORE CARE OF GOD.
       (Romans 5:8-10)

26.   I AM HIS INHERITANCE.
       (Ephesians 1:18)

27.   I HAVE AN INHERITANCE IN GOD.
       (1 Peter 1:4)

28.   I HAVE THE LIGHT OF THE LORD.
       (Ephesians 5:8)

29.   I AM VITALLY UNITED TO THE FATHER, THE SON,
       AND THE HOLY SPIRIT.
       (1 Thessalonians 1:1, Ephesians 4:6, Romans 8:1,
       John 14:20, Romans 8:9, 1 Corinthians 2:12)

30.   I AM BLESSED WITH THE FIRST FRUITS, OR THE
       EARNEST, OF THE HOLY SPIRIT.
       (2 Corinthians 1:22)

31.   I AM GLORIFIED.
       (Romans 8:18)

32.   I AM COMPLETE IN HIM.
       (Colossians 2:9-10)

33. I POSSESS EVERY SPIRITUAL BLESSING.
(Ephesians 1:3)

Lewis Sperry Chafer, *Systematic Theology, Volume III* (Dallas Seminary Press, 1948), 234-266.

ACKNOWLEDGMENTS

When my father, Dr. Herbert E. Kann, retired from forty years as a Presbyterian minister he gave me the books he valued most. Among them was his eight volume series of Systematic Theology authored by Dr. Lewis Sperry Chafer.

Dr. Chafer was an American theologian who founded the Dallas Theological Seminary and became its first president. Over a period of ten years he developed and completed his definitive work on Systematic Theology. From 1924 until his death in 1952, he served as president of that institution, and as professor of Systematic Theology. The function of Systematic Theology is to unfold in an orderly and methodical way the truths of Scripture. It is the study of God, and of man's relationship with Him.

My understanding of the life God offers to us and calls us to live has been greatly enhanced by Dr. Chafer's work. It is my prayer that this treatise has brought you a deeper knowledge and a fuller understanding of who God is, of why He loves you, and of the amazing provisions He has made for your life, both for today and for eternity!

It is with deep gratitude that I also express my appreciation to the following for their contributions:

To Eleanor Hanshaw, Barbara Haun, Lynda Hansard, Erin McKee, and Kelly Breedlove, who all brought their ideas and expertise to the project.

To my daughter, Lynn Talley, who designed the cover, edited the manuscript, and prepared it to go to press.

To my Thursday Bible Study Group. Thank you for your ongoing encouragement and prayers. Without your support the project could not have been completed.

NOTES

"God Cannot Accept You As you Are"
Lewis Sperry Chafer, *Systematic Theology, Volume II* (Dallas: Dallas Seminary Press, 1947), 224-273.

"However, God Has A Divine Plan"
Lewis Sperry Chafer, *Systematic Theology, Volume II* (Dallas: Dallas Seminary Press, 1947), 325-359 and *Volume VI*, 236-250.

"How Would God's Plan Be Fulfilled?"
J. Vernon McGee, *Thru The Bible, Volume IV* (Pasadena: Thru The Bible With J. Vernon McGee, 1983), 482-486.

"How Can This New Life Become Yours?"
Margaret Tadlock Kann, *Lessons of the Christian Life* (Fort Worth: Stillwater Books, A Division of Sycamore Creek Press, 2015), 428.

Lewis Sperry Chafer, *Systematic Theology, Volume III* (Dallas Seminary Press, 1948), 378-380.

"If You Accept This New Life, What Happens To You?"
Lewis Sperry Chafer, *Systematic Theology, Volume III* (Dallas Seminary Press), 62-72 and 328-331.

"Yet You Still Sin"
Lewis Sperry Chafer, *Systematic Theology, Volume II* (Dallas Seminary Press, 1947), 236-242.

"And The Best Is Yet To Come"
Lewis Sperry Chafer, *Systematic Theology, Volume II* (Dallas Seminary Press, 1947), 149-157.

"What Will Happen If You Reject God's Gift Of A New Birth?"
Lewis Sperry Chafer, *Systematic Theology, Volume IV* (Dallas Seminary Press, 1983), 427-433.

Bible Translations:

The King James Translation. Public domain.

The Living Bible. Copyright © 1971 by Tyndale House Publishers, Wheaton, Illinois, 60187. All rights reserved. Used by permission.

The Message; the Bible in Contemporary Language. Copyright © 1993, 1994, 1995, 1996, 2000. 2001, 2002. Used by permission of NavPress Publishing Group.

The New International Version, Copyright © 1988, 1989, 1990, 1991, by Tyndale House Publishers, Inc., Wheaton, Illinois, and from Zondervan Publishing House, Grand Rapids, Michigan. Used by permission. All rights reserved worldwide.

The New Testament in Modern English, translated by J.B. Phillips, Copyright © 1958, 1959, 1960, 1972 by J.B. Phillips. The Macmillan Company, New York, New York. Used by permission.

The Revised Standard Version, copyright © 1946 and 1971. Division of Christian Education of the National Council of Churches of Christ in the United States of America. Collins' Clear-type press. New York and Glascow. Used by permission.

Recommended Reading:

McDowell, Josh. *The Best of Josh McDowell: A Ready Defense.* Nashville: Thomas Nelson Inc.,1993.

McDowell, Josh. *The New Evidence That Demands A Verdict.* Nashville: Thomas Nelson Inc., 1999.

Strobel, Lee. *The Case for Christ.* Grand Rapids: Zondervan Publishing House, 1998.

Books by Marjorie Kann Jackson available on Amazon.com and Createspace.com:

Jackson, Marjorie Kann. *Blessings of the Christian Life.*
*This book proposes to lay out very basic information about the purpose of Christ coming to earth, and about what life is like when we allow Christ to live in and through us.

Jackson, Marjorie Kann. *Blessings of the Holy Spirit.*
*This book explains how the coming of the Holy Spirit is a crucial part of being born again, created anew for a spiritual life that is now one with God for eternity.

Jackson, Marjorie Kann. *The Journey.*
*Experience in a new way the glorious promise of Christmas. You will find your own story here as you journey with Mary and Joseph from Nazareth to Bethlehem.

Jackson, Marjorie Kann. *The Unavoidable Choice.*

Kann, Margaret Tadlock. *Lessons of the Christian Life.* Compiled by Marjorie Kann Jackson.
*A historical collection of Biblical truths as they appeared in the Fort Worth Star Telegram newspaper in the 1960s. These are lessons that will touch your soul, renew your mind, and fill your spirit.

* * *

Please visit us at Stillwaterbooksus.com or on our Facebook site, Stillwaterbooks.

28368514R00026

Made in the USA
Lexington, KY
14 January 2019